Gilson Araujo

PLANNING, TIME MANAGEMENT
PROSPERITY

"This e-book offers a practical and inspiring approach for Christian business leaders, combining biblical principles with effective strategies for overcoming limiting beliefs, managing time wisely, and achieving a life of abundance and sustainable success."

Gilson Araujo

Gilson Araujo has been a dedicated pastor and minister of the Gospel for over 20 years. Married to Fabiana Braz, he is a loving father of three girls and 10-year-old Pedro Dominic. He is the founder and president of Restaura-me Church, a church committed to expanding the kingdom of God, whose objective is to win souls, serve the community and restore lives.

In addition to his pastoral ministry, Gilson is a respected teacher and speaker. His academic background includes degrees in Law, Administration and Theology, a master's degree in Education and a specialization in Public Management. His passion for teaching and leadership led him to found the Jheset Seminary, as well as the Prosperus Business program, which aims to train and prepare businesspeople and entrepreneurs to successfully face their challenges.

With a clear vision and a practical approach, Gilson Araujo is dedicated to inspiring and empowering individuals, families and communities to reach their full potential in Christ. His experience and knowledge are valuable resources for those seeking guidance and spiritual growth.

Introduction: Chapter "Biblical Principles of Prosperity"

In the world of business and leadership, limiting beliefs are invisible barriers that many Christians face, often without realizing it. This chapter explores how these beliefs can obstruct the path to growth and prosperity, preventing pastors, leaders, and entrepreneurs from reaching the next level of success. Through powerful biblical examples, such as those of Joseph, Moses and David, we show how unshakable faith can transform adversity into opportunities for abundance. Additionally, we present statistical data and practical strategies to identify and overcome these mental barriers, renewing the mind and adopting a prosperity mindset. Discover how biblical principles can free you from self-imposed limitations and open the way to a life of success and fulfillment, according to God's will.

Introduction: Chapter "The Leader and Time Management"

Time management is one of the biggest challenges facing Christian leaders and entrepreneurs in today's fast-paced world. This chapter offers a practical, biblically grounded approach to helping leaders maximize their effectiveness and productivity without sacrificing their spiritual values and priorities. We explore biblical principles of wisdom and discernment, highlighting the importance of balancing professional and personal responsibilities. Through examples of biblical figures such as Nehemiah and Jesus, who exemplified effective time management, we show how to prioritize tasks, delegate responsibilities and reserve time for rest and spiritual reflection. Equipped with practical tools and techniques, you will learn to manage your time in ways that glorify God and propel your ministry and business to new heights of success.

Conclusion

This e-book is a practical and inspiring guide for Christian business leaders seeking to reach new heights of success, guided by the eternal principles of God's Word. From overcoming limiting beliefs to mastering time management, each chapter offers valuable insights, biblical examples, and practical strategies to transform your approach to business and personal life. Prepare for a journey of growth and prosperity that will align your faith with your business aspirations, leading you to a life of abundance and lasting impact.

CHAPTER I

BIBLICAL PRINCIPLES OF PROSPERITY

Chapter Summary: "Biblical Principles of Prosperity"

Prosperity in the life of a Christian, whether they are a leader, pastor, or entrepreneur, is a divine blessing meant for all children of God. This chapter explores how the path to prosperity is grounded in Scripture, demonstrating that God's will is for His children to prosper so they can bless the nations of the world. Often, limiting beliefs about wealth can hinder Christians from reaching their full potential. However, by understanding and applying biblical principles of prosperity, it is possible to transform these beliefs and open doors to a life of abundance and positive impact.

Part 1: Fundamentals of Christian Prosperity

Introduction

In the pursuit of prosperity in business and life, many Christians face unique challenges. In this chapter, we will explore how biblical principles can guide and strengthen Christian business leaders and entrepreneurs. We will delve into teachings that blend practical wisdom with a spiritual perspective to achieve sustainable success.

1. Christian Leadership and Business Vision

Defining a vision based on Christian faith principles

Christian leadership requires defining a vision that is aligned with faith principles. A faith-based vision is not just a statement of intentions but a clear direction grounded in biblical teachings. A Christian leader should seek God's guidance, praying and meditating on Scripture to discern the direction God wants their business to take. This vision should reflect values such as integrity, justice, and service to others, promoting a positive impact on society.

How inspirational leadership can positively impact the team and clients

Inspirational leadership is one that not only guides but motivates and transforms. Christian leaders are called to be examples of character and compassion, influencing their teams through service and love for others. They should demonstrate the fruits of the Spirit, such as patience, kindness, and self-control, creating a work environment where the team feels valued and motivated to achieve their full potential. Customers also perceive and value these qualities, which can strengthen loyalty and the company's reputation.

Case Study: Biblical examples of leaders who turned adverse circumstances into growth opportunities

The Bible is filled with examples of leaders who turned adversity into opportunities. Joseph, for example, faced betrayal by his brothers and unjust imprisonment but maintained his faith in God. With wisdom and integrity, he interpreted Pharaoh's dreams, helping Egypt prepare for famine, and was elevated to a position of great responsibility. Another example is Nehemiah, who, faced with the desolation of Jerusalem, gathered the exiles to rebuild the city walls, inspiring them with his faith and determination.

2. Entrepreneurship in the Light of the Word

Identifying business opportunities aligned with Christian values

Christian entrepreneurs should seek business opportunities that are in harmony with their faith values. This means not only avoiding unethical practices but also seeking ways to serve others through their products or services. Businesses that promote social justice, care for the environment, and community well-being are examples of aligning opportunities with Christian values.

Ethical business practices and their importance in Christian witness

Ethical business practices are crucial for Christian witness. Practices such as honesty, transparency, and accountability are essential for building trust with customers, partners, and employees. Companies that operate with integrity reflect Christ's teachings and can become a beacon in a business world often marked by corruption and greed.

Reflection: How Christian faith influences strategic decisions and organizational culture

Christian faith deeply influences strategic decisions and organizational culture. Decisions regarding partnerships, investments, and expansion should be made with prayer and seeking God's will. The organizational culture should promote an environment of respect, cooperation, and personal development, reflecting biblical principles. This approach not only honors God but also creates a solid foundation for sustainable business growth.

3. Innovation and Purpose-Driven Marketing

Innovating based on market needs and divine guidance

Innovation is crucial for business success, and Christian leaders can find inspiration in both market needs and divine guidance. God grants wisdom and creativity to develop solutions that meet market demands while promoting the common good. Innovation guided by Christian values seeks not only profit but also positive impact on society.

Marketing strategies that promote Christian values and the company's mission

Purpose-driven marketing is a powerful tool for communicating the company's values and mission. Marketing strategies should be transparent, honest, and reflect the company's commitment to ethics and social responsibility. Campaigns that promote Christian values such as compassion, justice, and sustainability can create a deeper connection with customers, strengthen the brand, and expand its reach.

Case Study: Entrepreneurs who combined creativity with integrity to achieve sustainable success

There are many examples of Christian entrepreneurs who have achieved success by combining creativity with integrity. One such story is that of Starbucks, the coffee company, whose CEO Howard Schultz has always emphasized the importance of treating employees and customers with respect and dignity. While not openly declaring itself as a Christian company, its principles of ethics and social responsibility reflect many Christian values.

Conclusion

This first part establishes the essential foundations for thriving as a Christian business leader. In the upcoming topics, we will explore each of these themes in more detail, providing practical tools and inspiring examples for immediate application. Prepare to transform your approach in business and reach new heights of success based on Biblical teachings.

Part 2: Christian Business Practices for Sustainable Success

Introduction

In this part, we will delve deeper into business practices that promote both success and Christian integrity. We will learn how to apply biblical principles in a practical and effective manner to thrive in business while witnessing our faith.

1. Business Ethics and Social Responsibility

The importance of integrity and transparency in business

Integrity and transparency are fundamental pillars for any company wishing to build a solid and lasting reputation. For Christian entrepreneurs, these qualities are even more essential as they directly reflect Christ's teachings. Integrity involves acting fairly and honestly in all situations, while transparency entails open and sincere communication with all stakeholders. Companies that value these practices gain the trust of customers, employees, and partners, creating a solid foundation for sustainable growth.

How Christian businesses can positively impact their communities

Christian businesses play a crucial role in the social and economic transformation of their communities. By adopting ethical and responsible business practices, they can provide dignified jobs, support social initiatives, and contribute to the overall well-being of the community. Investing in social responsibility projects such as education, health, and community development programs not only enhances the company's image but also aligns its activities with biblical principles of loving one's neighbor and service.

Case Study: Companies that adopted social responsibility policies based on biblical principles

A notable example is The Body Shop, a cosmetics company founded by Anita Roddick. Although not explicitly Christian, the company has a strong ethic of social responsibility that reflects many Christian values, such as respect for human dignity and environmental protection. The Body Shop has stood out for its campaigns against animal testing and promotion of fair trade, demonstrating how companies can adopt responsible policies that benefit society and the planet.

2. Financial Management with Wisdom

Biblical principles for personal and business financial management

The Bible offers various teachings on financial management, emphasizing the importance of wisdom, planning, and generosity. Proverbs 21:5, for example, states: "The plans of the diligent lead surely to abundance, but everyone who is hasty comes only to poverty." Christian business leaders should practice prudent financial administration, avoiding excessive debt and making wise investments. Generosity is also a key principle, with Malachi 3:10 encouraging the practice of tithing and offerings as a means of receiving blessings.

Strategies to achieve financial stability and sustainable growth

To achieve financial stability, it is essential to adopt practices such as detailed budgeting, constant financial monitoring, and creating emergency reserves. Sustainable growth can be achieved through careful investments, innovation, and strategic expansion. Companies should also seek to diversify their revenue sources and invest in the training and continuous development of their employees.

Reflection: How faith influences financial decisions and business investments

Christian faith can influence financial decisions by promoting a long-term perspective and an ethical focus in business. Investment decisions should consider not only financial returns but also social and environmental impact. Christian entrepreneurs are called to be faithful stewards of the resources entrusted to them by God, using them to promote good and help those in need.

3. Growth and Expansion Guided by Faith

Strategic planning in light of Christian principles

Strategic planning guided by faith involves seeking divine guidance at every stage of the growth and expansion process. This can be done through prayer, meditation on Scripture, and consultation with spiritual advisors. Psalm 37:5 advises, "Commit your way to the Lord; trust in him, and he will act." This principle suggests that business leaders should submit their plans to God, trusting that He will guide their steps to success.

How to Face Challenges and Crises with Faith and Resilience

Challenges and crises are inevitable in the business world, but faith can provide the strength needed to overcome them. Romans 5:3-4 teaches that tribulation produces perseverance, character, and hope. Christian business leaders should cultivate a resilient mindset, maintaining confidence in God even in difficult times. Strategies such as creating contingency plans and building a supportive organizational culture can help the company navigate crises successfully.

Case Study: Entrepreneurs who expanded their businesses based on spiritual principles

An example is Truett Cathy, founder of the Chick-fil-A fast food chain. Cathy based his business on Christian principles, such as closing the restaurants on Sundays to allow employees to rest and attend religious services. Despite losing a potential day of sales, this practice helped build a strong and loyal corporate culture, contributing to the company's success and continuous expansion.

Conclusion

This part offers valuable insights into applying Christian principles in business management to achieve sustainable growth and positively impact the business world. In the upcoming topics, we will continue to explore practical strategies to thrive as Christian business leaders. Prepare to transform your approach in business and reach new levels of success based on Biblical teachings.

Part 3: Innovation and Inspirational Leadership

Introduction

In this part, we will explore how innovation and inspirational leadership can drive business success and reflect fundamental Christian values. We will learn how to apply biblical principles to catalyze innovation and lead with excellence.

1. Innovation Based on Principles

The role of creativity and innovation in Christian businesses

Creativity and innovation are gifts from God that can be used to solve problems and create new opportunities. Christian businesses should encourage innovation that not only seeks profit but also serves the common good. By fostering an environment where creativity is valued and ideas are freely shared, business leaders can develop innovative solutions that meet market needs and honor God.

How to Identify Innovation Opportunities Aligned with the Company's Mission and Values

Identifying innovation opportunities requires a deep understanding of the company's mission and values. Companies should seek innovations that align with their ethical and spiritual principles, promoting community well-being and environmental stewardship. This can be achieved through market research, customer feedback, and continuous seeking of divine guidance.

Case Study: Examples of Companies that Innovated Based on Biblical Principles

An example is TOMS Shoes, which implemented the "One for One" model – for every pair of shoes sold, the company donates a pair to a child in need. This innovative business model not only promotes social responsibility but also reflects the biblical principle of helping the less fortunate.

2. Transformational Leadership

Leadership practices that reflect the teachings of Christ

Transformational leadership is not just about leading, but transforming those around you. Jesus is the supreme example of a transformational leader, as He served and empowered His disciples to become leaders themselves. Christian business leaders should follow His example by adopting practices of service, empathy, and empowerment. This includes active listening, supporting personal and professional development of employees, and leading with integrity and love.

How to inspire and empower teams with Christian values

Inspiration and empowerment are crucial for team success. Leaders should create an environment where Christian values such as respect, honesty, and cooperation are promoted and practiced. Encouraging active participation from employees, recognizing and celebrating their contributions, and providing opportunities for growth and continuous development are ways to empower the team.

Reflection: How transformational leadership can positively influence organizational culture

Transformational leadership has the potential to transform organizational culture, creating an environment of trust, collaboration, and innovation. An organizational culture based on Christian principles attracts and retains talent, enhances employee motivation and engagement, and strengthens the company's reputation. Leaders who exemplify Christ's teachings in their daily actions inspire others to do the same, generating a lasting positive impact.

3. Purpose-Driven Marketing Strategies

Developing Marketing Strategies that Promote Christian Values

Effective marketing strategies should reflect the company's Christian values, promoting honesty, transparency, and responsibility. This can include campaigns that highlight the company's commitment to social justice, sustainability, and service to others. Purpose-driven marketing is more than just selling products – it's about telling the company's story and its positive impact on the world.

The Impact of Christian Witness on Brand Reputation and Customer Relations

Christian witness can have a significant impact on brand reputation and customer relations. When a company operates with transparency, integrity, and social responsibility, this is reflected in a positive image to the public. Customers tend to trust companies more when they demonstrate a genuine commitment to ethical principles and Christian values. This not only builds loyalty among existing customers but also attracts new consumers who share these values.

Case Study: Companies that Integrated Purpose-Driven Marketing to Reach a Wider Audience

An example is the organic food company Ben & Jerry's. While not explicitly Christian, the company adopts marketing practices that reflect values such as social justice, sustainability, and respect for others. Their campaigns often address issues like climate justice and fair trade, demonstrating how purpose-driven marketing can engage and expand the customer base.

Conclusion

This part highlights the importance of innovation, inspirational leadership, and purpose-driven marketing within the Christian business context. In the upcoming chapters, we will continue to explore how these principles can be practically applied to promote sustainable growth and build a business community based on faith.

Part 4: Overcoming Challenges and Growing in Wisdom

Introduction

In this part, we will explore how Christian business leaders can face challenges with faith and wisdom, while cultivating a mindset of lasting prosperity. We will learn how to apply biblical principles to overcome adversities and grow in all areas of business life.

1. **Resilience and Faith in Times of Crisis**

Maintaining Faith and Hope in the Face of Business Challenges

Maintaining faith and hope during business crises is essential to overcoming adversities. Christian leaders should trust in God, seeking His guidance and strength through prayer and meditation on the Word. Biblical passages like Isaiah 41:10, which says "Fear not, for I am with you; be not dismayed, for I am your God; I will strengthen you, I will help you, I will uphold you with my righteous right hand," offer comfort, certainty, and encouragement.

Strategies for Cultivating Personal and Organizational Resilience

Cultivating resilience involves developing a positive and proactive mindset. Leaders should encourage their team to see challenges as opportunities for growth and learning. Practices such as creating contingency plans, promoting a supportive environment, and offering continuous training can strengthen organizational resilience. Additionally, fostering a culture of gratitude and celebrating small victories helps maintain morale during tough times.

Case Study: Examples of Leaders Who Faced Crises Based on Christian Principles

An inspiring story is that of Dave Ramsey, a Christian financial counselor who faced bankruptcy in the 1980s. Ramsey rebuilt his career and created a financial consulting firm based on biblical principles of financial management. Today, he helps millions of people manage their finances wisely and ethically, demonstrating how faith and resilience can turn crises into opportunities for ministry and success.

2. **Personal and Professional Development**

The Importance of Continuous Growth in the Business Journey

Continuous personal and professional development is crucial for any leader who wishes to thrive. The Bible encourages growth and the pursuit of wisdom, as in Proverbs 4:7: "The beginning of wisdom is this: Get wisdom, and whatever you get, get insight." Leaders should invest in their own development and that of their employees, promoting a culture of continuous learning.

Practices to Develop Effective Leadership and Management Skills

To develop leadership and management skills, leaders can participate in training, workshops, and mentoring programs. Additionally, reading books on Christian leadership, participating in business-focused Bible study groups, and seeking advice from other Christian leaders are valuable practices. Self-awareness and reflection are also important for identifying areas for improvement and growth.

Reflection: How the pursuit of wisdom and knowledge can strengthen the foundation for business success The pursuit of wisdom and knowledge strengthens the foundation for business success by enabling leaders to make informed and ethical decisions. The Bible, in James 1:5, encourages us to ask God for wisdom, which he generously gives. Leaders who dedicate themselves to continuous learning and the application of biblical principles are better prepared to face challenges and seize growth opportunities.

3. The Path to Prosperity in Light of the Bible

Biblical principles for achieving true prosperity

True prosperity, according to the Bible, goes beyond material success and includes spiritual and emotional well-being. Principles such as integrity (Proverbs 10:9), diligence (Proverbs 13:4), and generosity (2 Corinthians 9:6-8) are foundational. Additionally, Jesus teaches us to seek first the Kingdom of God and His righteousness, trusting that all other things will be added to us (Matthew 6:33).

Balancing material success with an enriching spiritual life

Balancing material success with an enriching spiritual life requires prioritizing the relationship with God in all areas of life. This includes setting aside time for prayer, Bible study, and fellowship with other believers. Leaders should also practice gratitude and generosity, recognizing that everything they possess is a gift from God and should be used for His glory and to help others.

Case Study: Entrepreneurs who found a sustainable balance between material prosperity and spirituality

Mary Kay Ash, founder of Mary Kay Cosmetics, is an example of an entrepreneur who balanced material success with spirituality. She based her company on Christian principles, promoting the Golden Rule and encouraging her consultants to prioritize faith, family, and career in that order. This balance was one of the factors contributing to the enduring success of her company.

Conclusion

This section emphasizes the importance of resilience, personal and spiritual development, and the path to true prosperity according to biblical principles. In the upcoming chapters, we will continue to explore how these principles can be applied to transform businesses and lives, following divine guidance.

Part 5: Overcoming Limiting Beliefs to Achieve Abundance

Introduction

In this section, we will address a crucial theme for the growth and prosperity of Christian business leaders: limiting beliefs. Often, these beliefs hinder pastors, leaders, and Christian entrepreneurs from reaching the next level of success and abundance. We will explore how to identify and overcome these mental barriers, demonstrating that they are artificial impediments that can be overcome with faith, wisdom, and action.

1.What Are Limiting Beliefs?

Limiting beliefs are thoughts and convictions that restrict our actions and possibilities. They form over time, often from negative experiences, cultural influences, and misunderstandings of teachings. In the Christian context, some of these beliefs may seem spiritually grounded but actually distort God's purpose for our lives.

Common Examples of Limiting Beliefs

1. "Money is the root of all evil": This is a misinterpretation of 1 Timothy 6:10, which actually states that the love of money is the root of all evils. Wealth, when acquired and used wisely, can be a powerful tool for good.
2. "Being humble means being poor": Humility is not synonymous with poverty. Jesus calls us to be humble in heart (Matthew 11:29), but this does not imply renouncing financial success.
3. "I cannot be successful and spiritual at the same time": Success and spirituality are not mutually exclusive. Joseph and Daniel, for example, were highly successful and deeply spiritual.

2.The Impact of Limiting Beliefs

Limiting beliefs can have a devastating impact on personal and professional life. They can lead to stagnation, lack of motivation, and a distorted view of divine purpose. Studies show that people with limiting beliefs are more likely to experience low levels of satisfaction and success.

Statistical Data

A study from Stanford University revealed that 80% of individuals who believe in their abilities are more likely to achieve financial and personal success. In contrast, those with limiting beliefs often face obstacles that hinder their progress.

3.Overcoming Limiting Beliefs

Identification and Deconstruction

The first step in overcoming limiting beliefs is to identify them. This involves introspection and often seeking feedback from mentors or spiritual leaders. Once identified, these beliefs must be deconstructed and replaced with biblical truths.

1 Reflection and Prayer: Ask God to reveal areas in your life where limiting beliefs may be operating.

2 Study of the Word: Meditate on Bible verses that contradict these limiting beliefs. For example, Philippians 4:13 states: "I can do all things through him who strengthens me."

3 Action and Confidence: Take practical steps to challenge these beliefs. If you believe you cannot lead a large company, start equipping yourself and seeking opportunities that expand your leadership.

Biblical Examples of Overcoming

Example 1: Joseph

Joseph was sold as a slave but never let that limit his vision for the future. He kept his faith in God and eventually became the second most powerful man in Egypt. His story teaches us that regardless of circumstances, God can elevate us to levels of abundance and success.

Example 2: Moses

Moses faced numerous challenges throughout his life, from being hidden for three months as a baby to fleeing Egypt after killing an Egyptian. Despite his failures and fears, God called him to lead the Israelites out of slavery. Moses overcame his limiting beliefs of inadequacy and fear, trusting in divine guidance, and became one of the greatest leaders in biblical history, guiding the Israelites through the desert towards the Promised Land.

Example 3: David

David started his life as a simple shepherd and faced many challenges, including fighting the giant Goliath and being persecuted by King Saul. His unwavering faith in God allowed him to overcome these adversities and eventually become the king of Israel. David teaches us that with courage and confidence in God, we can overcome any obstacle and achieve great feats, even when our initial circumstances seem unfavorable.

These examples demonstrate that, regardless of circumstances and challenges, faith in God can elevate us to levels of abundance and success, overcoming any limiting beliefs.

4.The Path to Abundance

Renewal of the Mind

Romans 12:2 exhorts us not to conform to this world, but to be transformed by the renewal of our mind. This transformation is crucial for abandoning limiting beliefs and adopting a mindset of abundance.

Continuous Development Investing in education, training, and personal development is essential. Leaders who continually seek growth are more likely to overcome mental barriers and achieve their goals.

Supportive Community Surrounding oneself with a supportive community that shares the same faith and vision can be a powerful catalyst for change. Participating in Bible study groups, Christian business seminars, and networking events can provide the encouragement and perspective needed.

Conclusion Limiting beliefs are artificial barriers that hinder us from reaching the full potential God has given us. By identifying and overcoming these beliefs, we can pave the way for a life of abundance and prosperity according to biblical principles. Remember the words of Jesus in John 10:10: "I came that they may have life and have it abundantly."

May we all break free from these limiting beliefs and embrace the abundant life that God has planned for us. As Christian business leaders, we have the calling and ability to positively influence the world around us, reflecting God's glory in all our actions.

Part 6: Consolidating Principles for Lasting Prosperity

Introduction

In this final part, we will consolidate the learnings on how Christian business leaders can apply biblical principles to achieve sustainable prosperity and build a business community grounded in faith. We will learn how to integrate all aspects discussed throughout this chapter for effective transformation in business and personal life.

1.Integration of Values and Business Mission

Aligning Company Values with the Christian Mission

Aligning company values with the Christian mission involves incorporating biblical principles into all operational areas. The mission should reflect a commitment to justice, integrity, and service to others. Companies can create mission statements that emphasize these values and ensure that all policies and practices are in line with them. This includes hiring employees who share these values and implementing corporate social responsibility programs.

Strategies to maintain business integrity and coherence

Maintaining integrity and coherence requires constant vigilance and exemplary leadership. Leaders must establish and maintain high ethical standards, act transparently, and hold all members of the organization accountable for their actions. Regular audits, open feedback and a culture of honest communication are effective strategies to ensure the company remains true to its values.

Case study: Companies that have integrated Christian values into all areas of their operations

The healthcare company Johnson & Johnson, although not explicitly Christian, exemplifies how ethical values and social responsibility can be integrated into all areas of operations. Its credo emphasizes responsibility to patients, doctors, nurses, staff and the community, reflecting many Christian values.

2. Community Impact and Christian Witness

The role of Christian businesses in social and cultural transformation

Christian businesses play a vital role in social and cultural transformation. They can serve as agents of change, promoting social justice, sustainability and care for the less privileged. This can be done through partnerships with nonprofit organizations, supporting community initiatives, and promoting ethical business practices.

How to be a living testimony of the gospel through business

Being a living testimony to the gospel through business involves more than words – it involves actions. Companies must treat all stakeholders with respect and dignity, demonstrate generosity and fairness, and operate with integrity. Leaders must be examples of Christian character, inspiring others to follow the teachings of Christ in their own lives.

Reflection: Opportunities to positively influence the business environment and society

There are countless opportunities for Christian businesses to positively influence the business environment and society. Actively participating in community initiatives, offering mentoring and training programs, and supporting causes that promote social justice and sustainability are some of the ways companies can make a significant impact. Furthermore, by upholding ethical and transparent business practices, Christian companies can establish new standards of integrity in the business world.

3. Sustainable and Ethical Practices

The importance of environmental and social sustainability

Environmental and social sustainability is essential to ensure that business operations do not harm the environment or communities. Christian companies must lead by example, adopting practices that minimize environmental impact and promote social well-being. This includes responsible use of resources, reducing waste and implementing programs that benefit local communities.

Strategies for implementing sustainable business practices

Implementing sustainable business practices can involve several strategies, such as investing in green technologies, promoting the recycling and reuse of materials, and adopting ethical sourcing policies. Companies can also educate their employees about the importance of sustainability and encourage them to adopt responsible practices in their daily lives. Partnerships with other organizations and participation in global sustainability initiatives are also effective ways to make a positive impact.

Case study: Companies that lead in sustainability and social responsibility

Patagonia, an outdoor clothing and equipment company, is a notable example of its commitment to sustainability and social responsibility. The company is dedicated to environmentally responsible production practices and contributes a significant portion of its profits to environmental causes. This commitment not only reinforces the company's reputation, but also demonstrates how ethical values can guide business decisions and inspire positive change.

4. Planning for the Future with Faith

The importance of strategic planning for lasting prosperity

Strategic planning is crucial to ensuring a company's lasting prosperity. Christian business leaders should seek divine guidance when setting long-term goals and strategies, trusting God to guide them in their decisions. Planning must consider not only financial objectives, but also how the company can continue to positively impact society and the environment.

How to set goals and objectives aligned with Christian principles

Setting goals and objectives aligned with Christian principles involves considering the impact of business actions on all stakeholders and ensuring that the company's activities reflect values such as integrity, justice and service to others. Leaders must involve their team in the goal-setting process, promoting a culture of collaboration and commitment to ethical principles.

Reflection: Trust in God to guide the company's future

Trusting God to guide the company's future means recognizing that while planning and human effort are important, it is divine providence that ultimately determines success. In Proverbs 16:3 we read: "Commit your works to the Lord, and your plans will be established." Leaders must constantly seek God's guidance, remaining open to His will and willing to adjust their plans as necessary.

5. Conclusion: A Call to Action

Recap of the principles covered

Throughout this chapter, we explore how biblical principles can be applied to promote success and integrity in business. We discuss the importance of ethics and social responsibility, wise financial management, innovation and transformational leadership, resilience and continuous growth, sustainability and strategic planning. Each of these topics provides a solid foundation for building a prosperous company aligned with Christian values.

An invitation to continuous transformation

This chapter is an invitation to continuous transformation – not just of business, but also of the hearts and minds of business leaders. As we apply biblical principles in our lives and businesses, we are called to be a light in the business world, positively influencing our communities and witnessing the love of Christ through our actions.

A future of prosperity and positive impact

By integrating these principles into our business practices, we can achieve a future of prosperity and positive impact. By trusting God and seeking His guidance in all areas of our lives, we have the opportunity to create companies that not only prosper financially, but also contribute to a more just, ethical and compassionate world. May we be leaders who reflect the light of Christ in all our actions, building a legacy of faith, hope and love.

CHAPTER II
THE LEADER AND TIME MANAGEMENT

Chapter Summary: "The leader and Time Management"

In this chapter, we explore the importance of time management for leaders, pastors, and business owners, highlighting key practices and principles that can transform the way they manage their daily activities. Based on the theories and methods of renowned authors such as Jake Knapp, John Zeratsky, Stephen R. Covey, Christian Barbosa and Cristine Carter, we offer a practical guide to optimize time, increase productivity and achieve a healthy work-life balance.

INTRODUCTION

Time is the most valuable and finite resource we have. As leaders, how we manage our time not only impacts our personal effectiveness, but also directly influences the effectiveness of our organizations and communities. This chapter aims to provide a practical and inspired roadmap for leaders who want to maximize their impact through efficient and strategic time management. We'll explore essential concepts, proven strategies, and daily practices that can help transform your approach to time.

Part 1: Understanding the Importance of Time Management

The Relationship between Time and Leadership

Effective leadership requires a deep understanding of the value of time. Stephen R. Covey highlights in his book "The 7 Habits of Highly Effective People" that leaders must focus on what is important, not just what is urgent. Understanding this distinction is crucial for prioritizing tasks that bring long-term value.

The Impact of Time Management on Productivity

Christian Barbosa, in "The Triad of Time", teaches us that time, energy and attention are interdependent. Leaders who learn to manage these three elements in an integrated way are able to significantly increase their productivity and that of their teams. The ability to plan, delegate and focus on high-impact activities is what sets successful leaders apart.

Time as a Strategic Resource

Pastors and religious leaders often face unique challenges related to time management. The demand for pastoral care, sermon preparation, and church administration can be overwhelming. Here, time management becomes not just a matter of productivity, but also of spiritual and mental health. John Zeratsky and Jake Knapp, in "Make Time," emphasize the need to create rituals and routines that protect time for critical activities and self-care.

Part 2: Fundamentals of Time Management

The Eisenhower Matrix

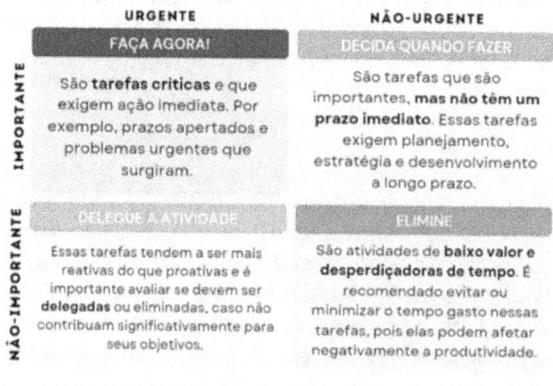

The Eisenhower Matrix, popularized by Stephen R. Covey, is an essential tool for leaders. It helps categorize tasks into four quadrants: urgent and important, non-urgent but important, urgent but not important, and neither urgent nor important. This tool helps leaders identify and focus on the tasks that really matter, avoiding the trap of spending time on activities that don't significantly contribute to their goals.

The Power of Focus and Priority

The ability to stay focused on the most important tasks is essential. Jake Knapp and John Zeratsky introduce the concept of "Highlight" in "Make Time," which involves choosing a top priority for the day and ensuring it gets the attention it needs. This simple yet powerful method can transform leaders' daily productivity.

Planning and Review

Cristian Barbosa suggests in "The Time Triad" that weekly planning is crucial for effective time management. Reviewing the previous week's goals, planning the following week's activities, and adjusting as needed helps leaders stay on track and adapt to inevitable changes.

Part 3: Daily Practices for Efficient Time Management

Morning and Evening Routines

Establishing morning and evening routines can be one of the most impactful time management habits. Stephen R. Covey talks about the importance of starting the day with a purpose, including time for reflection, planning, and preparation. Evening routines should include reviewing the day, planning for the next day, and time for relaxation.

Productivity Techniques

Techniques like Pomodoro, time blocks, and regular rest breaks can help maintain focus and energy throughout the day. These techniques are especially useful for pastors and leaders who need to balance administrative tasks with spiritual preparation and pastoral care.

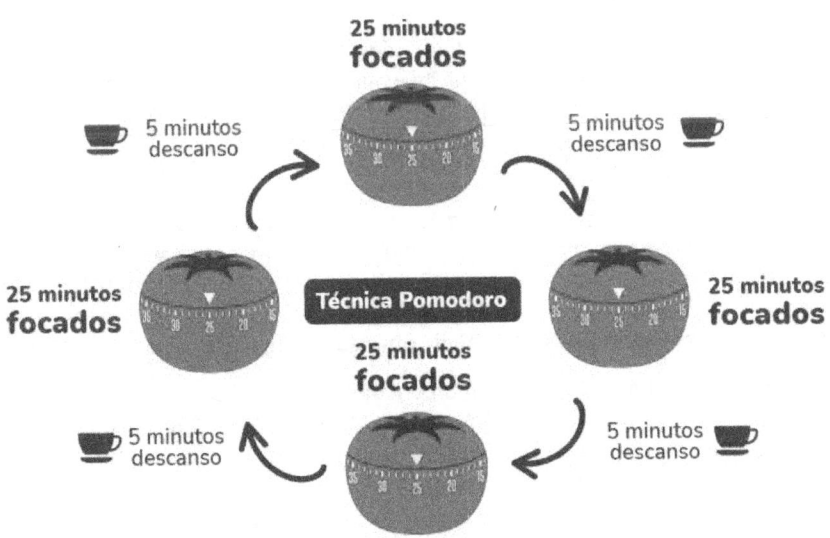

Delegation and Automation

Learning to delegate tasks is essential for any leader. Identifying activities that can be delegated to other team members or automated with the help of technology allows leaders to focus their time and energy on the tasks that truly require their attention.

Part 4: Work-Life Balance

Importance of Self-Care

Cristine Carter, in her work on happiness and productivity, highlights the importance of self-care for long-term effectiveness. Leaders must make time for activities that rejuvenate and maintain balance, such as exercise, hobbies and time with family.

Healthy Boundaries

Establishing clear boundaries between personal and professional life is vital. This includes setting work schedules, learning to say no to excessive commitments, and creating spaces for rest and disconnection.

Time for Spirituality

For pastors, time dedicated to prayer, Bible study, and spiritual reflection is non-negotiable. Ensuring these activities are integrated into your daily routine helps maintain the mental clarity and spiritual strength needed to lead effectively.

History and Analogies: The Overburdened Shepherd

Imagine the story of Pastor João, a dedicated leader of a small congregation in a busy city. Pastor João is known for his passion and dedication to the ministry. He spends countless hours serving church members, preparing inspiring sermons, and managing various community activities. However, Pastor João has one big flaw: he rarely takes time for himself or his family.

Weeks turn into months, and Pastor João begins to feel the signs of exhaustion. He finds himself constantly tired, his creativity wanes, and his patience runs out quickly. His family begins to notice his absence, and his friends barely see him. He believes he is making sacrifices for the good of his congregation, but in reality, he is neglecting the greatest resource he has: his time.

Pastor João's situation is comparable to a car that never receives maintenance. Imagine driving a car day after day, year after year, without ever stopping to change the oil, check the tires, or refill the tank. Eventually, the car will start to fail, no matter how new or strong it is. In the same way, Pastor João is directing his life and his ministry without stopping to "replenish" his physical, mental and spiritual energies.

Time is not money; time is life. Every moment that Pastor João neglects his well-being is a wasted moment, a piece of his life that he can never get back. As leaders, it is crucial to understand that we are not infinite. Our strengths, energy and creativity have limits that need to be respected.

By recognizing the importance of taking vacations, spending quality time with family and friends, and setting aside periods for leisure and rest, Pastor João can revitalize his life and ministry. He will learn that caring for himself is not a selfish act, but a responsibility he has to himself and his congregation. Just as a well-maintained car can run for many years, a leader who values and manages his time well can serve with passion and effectiveness throughout his life.

Conclusion

Time management is a vital skill for leaders, pastors and business owners. Implementing effective time management practices not only increases productivity, but also improves overall well-being and long-term impact. By following the principles and techniques discussed in this chapter, leaders can transform their approach to time, ensuring that their actions are aligned with their highest values and goals. This way, they will be able to lead more effectively, inspire their teams and achieve a healthy balance between their professional and personal responsibilities.

Remember, time is not money. Time is life. And as leaders, our responsibility is to live fully and intentionally, ensuring that every moment counts.

CHAPTER III

TAKE CARE OF YOUR EMOTIONS – A Theopsychological Analysis of Burnout Syndrome

Chapter Summary: "TAKE CARE OF YOUR EMOTIONS – A Theopsychological Analysis of Burnout Syndrome"

This chapter explores Burnout Syndrome from the perspective of Theopsychology, with a special focus on pastors who face emotional exhaustion due to their ministerial responsibilities. The aim is to provide an understanding of the condition, highlighting the intersection between Psychological Science and Christian Theology. Drawing inspiration from the teachings of Jesus and the insights of renowned authors and recent international research, we will discuss the nature, causes, symptoms, and prevention and treatment strategies for Burnout, emphasizing the importance of comprehensive care for human beings. This study aims to equip religious leaders and therapists with practical and spiritual tools for dealing with emotional burnout.

INTRODUCTION

Burnout Syndrome, characterized by extreme physical and emotional exhaustion, has become a growing concern in the contemporary world. Among the most vulnerable groups are pastors, whose emotional, spiritual and administrative demands can lead them to a state of severe exhaustion. Theopsychology, a field that integrates the principles of psychology with theology, offers a unique and powerful approach to understanding and treating this condition. Drawing inspiration from the teachings of Jesus and modern insights from psychology, we can develop effective strategies to prevent and treat Burnout, promoting the overall health of leaders.

There is growing concern about emotional exhaustion (Burnout) among pastors, both in Brazil and globally:

1. **High Consideration of Abandonment:** A significant number of pastors have considered abandoning the ministry. In the United States, 38% of pastors considered leaving full-time ministry in the last year, a notable increase compared to 29% at the beginning of 2021. This rate is even higher among younger pastors, with 46% of those under 45 years considering resignation (Barna Group) (Minister's Hub).

2. **Impact on Ministry and Congregations:** The post-pandemic era has compounded challenges for pastors, leading to increased burnout. A survey conducted in late 2023 found that about a third of clergy were considering leaving their congregations and ministry entirely (Religion News Service) (Baptist Press). Contributing factors include declining church attendance, volunteer fatigue and congregations' resistance to change (Religion News Service).

3. **Mental and Physical Health:** Only one in three pastors is considered healthy in terms of well-being, covering spiritual, physical, emotional, vocational and financial aspects. This reflects a growing crisis where many pastors are struggling significantly with burnout (Barna Group).

4. **Family and Personal Impact:** Pastors' families are also affected. About 80% of pastors believe their ministry has negatively impacted their families, with many pastors' children choosing not to attend church due to their parents' experiences (Minister's Hub).

5. **Global Context:** Although specific statistics for Brazil are less available, global trends indicate similar challenges. The pressures and expectations on pastors are universal, leading to significant mental health challenges and considerations of leaving the ministry.

These findings highlight the urgent need for proactive measures to support pastoralists. This includes fostering community support, encouraging rest and self-care, and addressing systemic issues within congregational life that contribute to burnout. The Church must support its leaders by offering prayer, practical assistance, and a renewed emphasis on well-being to ensure the sustainability and vitality of pastoral ministry.

Part 1: Understanding Burnout Syndrome

Definition and History

Burnout Syndrome was first described in the 1970s by psychologist Herbert Freudenberger. It has since become a widely recognized term to describe a condition of physical, emotional and mental exhaustion caused by prolonged stress and overwork. In theopsychology, Burnout is seen not only as a psychological phenomenon, but also a spiritual one, affecting the soul and the individual's purpose in life.

Symptoms and Diagnosis

Symptoms of burnout include extreme fatigue, cynicism, detachment, feelings of ineffectiveness and lack of accomplishment. In pastors, these symptoms can manifest as a loss of faith, difficulty connecting with the congregation, and a feeling of spiritual isolation. Diagnosis involves evaluating physical, emotional and behavioral signs, in addition to considering the individual's spiritual and ministerial context.

Causes and Risk Factors

Several factors contribute to the development of Burnout, including excessive workloads, lack of support, unrealistic expectations and internal conflicts. For pastors, the pressures of leading a community, providing ongoing spiritual support, and dealing with personal and congregational crises are significant risk factors.

Part 2: Theopsychology, the Teachings of Jesus and Neuroscience

Theopsychology as a Field of Study

Theopsychology combines the principles of psychology with Christian theology, offering a perspective that integrates body, soul and spirit. This approach recognizes that spiritual health is fundamental to psychological well-being and vice versa.

Jesus' Teachings on Comprehensive Care

Jesus, in His teachings, emphasized the importance of rest, fellowship, and self-care. He often withdrew to solitary places to pray and renew His spiritual and emotional strength. These principles are vital for preventing and treating Burnout.

The Role of Faith and Prayer

Faith and prayer offer a source of strength and resilience in times of stress. For pastors, connection with God and the practice of continuous prayer are essential resources for maintaining emotional health and preventing burnout.

The Effects of Prayer on the Brain and Emotions: Evidence from Neuroscience

Prayer, which should be the central practice in the life of any servant of God, especially pastors, has been the object of study in neuroscience due to its profound effects on the brain and, consequently, on emotions. Several scientific researches have demonstrated how prayer can positively influence the mental, emotional and even physical health of individuals. Things that the Bible has already told us for millennia, such as: (Ps 30.2; John 6.63b; James 5.16). In this topic we will check the neuroscientific discoveries about the effects of prayer on the human brain.

1. Activation of Specific Brain Areas

Prayer activates several regions of the brain associated with attention, emotion and self-control. Neuroimaging studies reveal that during prayer and meditation, areas such as the prefrontal cortex, responsible for concentration and planning, and the limbic system, which manages emotions, are particularly involved.

- **Prefrontal Cortex:** Involved in attention and concentration, the prefrontal cortex is highly active during prayer, indicating a state of focus and introspection (Barna Group).

- **Limbic System:** This region, which includes structures such as the amygdala and hippocampus, is responsible for emotional regulation. Activation of the limbic system during prayer suggests a link between spiritual practices and the management of emotions such as anxiety and stress (Barna Group).

2. Reducing Stress and Anxiety

Research shows that prayer can lower stress and anxiety levels. A study published in the "Journal of Behavioral Medicine" found that individuals who regularly practice prayer have lower levels of cortisol, the stress hormone.

- **Cortisol:** Regular prayer has been associated with a reduction in cortisol levels, promoting a state of calm and well-being (Barna Group).

3. Improved Emotional Health

The practice of prayer is linked to improvements in emotional health, including increased feelings of well-being, hope and happiness. Studies suggest that prayer can function as a form of cognitive behavioral therapy, helping individuals reframe negative thoughts and strengthen emotional resilience.

- **Emotional Resilience:** Prayer can help increase emotional resilience, providing a sense of support and spiritual connection that helps overcome adversity (Barna Group).

4. Changes in Brain Activity

Functional neuroimaging shows that prayer and meditation can lead to lasting changes in brain activity, particularly in areas related to emotional control and self-control. Functional magnetic resonance imaging (fMRI) studies indicate that people who pray regularly have a greater ability to regulate their emotions and maintain a calm state under pressure.

- **Neuroplasticity:** Prayer promotes neuroplasticity, the brain's ability to reorganize itself and form new neuronal connections, especially in response to regular spiritual practices (Barna Group).

5. Increased Empathy and Altruism

Prayer, especially intercessory, is associated with an increase in empathy and altruistic behaviors. This may be due to the activation of areas of the brain linked to compassion and understanding the suffering of others.

- **Compassion:** Prayer practices that involve thinking about others can increase activity in brain areas related to empathy, promoting feelings of compassion and altruism (Barna Group).

Pastor Pray, Neuroscience has revealed how prayer affects the brain in ways that can significantly improve mental and emotional health. The activation of specific areas of the brain, the reduction of stress and anxiety, the improvement of emotional health, changes in brain activity and increased empathy are some of the benefits proven by science. These findings underscore the importance of prayer as an integral practice for spiritual and psychological well-being, especially for those in positions of spiritual leadership, such as pastors, who face high levels of stress and responsibility.

These findings reinforce the need to integrate regular spiritual practices into pastoral care, promoting not only the emotional health of leaders but also strengthening their abilities to lead and support their faith communities.

Part 3: Prevention and Treatment Strategies

Self-knowledge and self-care

A deep understanding of yourself and your own limitations is crucial to preventing Burnout. Self-care practices, such as adequate rest, healthy nutrition, physical exercise and leisure time, are essential.

Social and Community Support

Support from friends, family and colleagues is essential. For pastors, building a support network inside and outside the church can provide a haven of renewal and encouragement.

Therapeutic Interventions

Cognitive behavioral therapy, acceptance and commitment therapy, and other psychological approaches can be effective in treating Burnout. The integration of spiritual practices, such as meditation on the word of God and prayer, can enhance therapeutic results.

The Role of the Church

The church can play a crucial role in supporting its leaders. Pastoral care programs, spiritual retreats, and a culture of compassion and understanding are vital to the health of pastors.

Burnout Syndrome is a painful reality for many pastors, but with a Theopsychological approach, we can offer hope and healing. By integrating the principles of psychology with the teachings of Jesus, we can develop effective strategies to prevent and treat emotional exhaustion. Faith, spirituality and comprehensive care are fundamental pillars for the health and well-being of ministers. By nourishing the body, mind, and spirit, we can help pastors find renewal and purpose while continuing to serve their communities with passion and vigor.

A Story: Pastor Miguel's Garden

The Blooming Garden

In a small town, there was a shepherd named Miguel. He was known for his compassionate heart and his tireless commitment to his congregation. Miguel had a beautiful garden, full of vibrant flowers and fruit trees. This garden was a reflection of his ministry life - a place where he found peace, renewal and inspiration.

Miguel dedicated hours a day to caring for his garden, ensuring that each plant received the right amount of water, sunlight and nutrients. He knew that to keep his garden healthy, he needed to be attentive to its needs.

The First Signs of Exhaustion

Over time, Miguel's responsibilities in the church increased. He was always available to meet the needs of his congregation, whether providing spiritual counseling, visiting the sick or organizing community events. The constant pressure started to take a toll on her gardening routine.

The first signs of exhaustion began to appear. The once vibrant flowers began to wither, and the fruit trees no longer produced fruit as abundantly. Miguel found himself so busy that he barely had time to rest or take care of himself.

The Abandoned Garden

As the months passed, Miguel's garden began to reflect his internal state. The weeds grew out of control, choking out the plants he loved so much. The land, once rich and fertile, was dry and cracked. Miguel felt tired, unmotivated and unable to find joy in the activities that previously brought him so much satisfaction.

His congregation also began to notice the changes. Michael's sermons, once full of passion and inspiration, became mechanical and lifeless. He felt disconnected from his faith and his community, and the weight of responsibilities seemed unbearable.

The Call to Self-Care

One day, Miguel's old friend, Pastor João, came to visit him. João immediately noticed the state of the garden and Miguel's haggard face. With wisdom and compassion, he said:

"Michael, your garden reflects the state of your soul. You are trying to take care of everyone, but you have forgotten to take care of yourself. Remember Jesus' teachings about rest and self-care. He said, 'Come to me, all you who are weary and burdened, and I will give you rest.'"

João suggested that Miguel take time to rest and renew his strength. He spoke about the importance of self-care, both physical and spiritual, and how this was essential to continuing to serve with passion and effectiveness.

The Renewal of the Garden and the Soul

Miguel decided to follow João's advice. He began to delegate some of his responsibilities at church and set aside time daily for rest and reflection. He returned to tending his garden, dedicating himself to pulling out the weeds, fertilizing the soil and watering the plants regularly.

Over time, the flowers began to bloom again, and the fruit trees began to produce abundant fruit again. Miguel's garden, now vibrant and healthy, became a symbol of his spiritual and emotional renewal.

Miguel also began to prioritize his mental and spiritual health. He devoted time to prayer, meditation, and study of the Scriptures. He set healthy boundaries around his work, ensuring he had time for activities that brought him joy and renewal.

Lessons from the Garden

Pastor Miguel's story teaches us about the causes and effects of Burnout Syndrome and the vital importance of self-care. Just as a garden needs constant care to flourish, we also need to take care of our physical, emotional and spiritual needs.

Spiritual leaders, like pastors, face unique pressures that can lead to burnout. It is essential to recognize the signs of Burnout and take proactive steps to prevent and treat this condition. Practicing self-care, establishing healthy limits and seeking social and spiritual support are fundamental to maintaining health and well-being.

By caring for themselves, pastors not only renew their own strength but also become living examples for their congregations, showing that comprehensive care is a crucial component of a full and abundant life.

www.ingramcontent.com/pod-product-compliance
Lightning Source LLC
Chambersburg PA
CBHW072057230526
45479CB00010B/1128